William Richert, Robin Tate and Kevin Chamberlin in a scene from the McCarter Theatre production of "Pvt. Wars."

PVT. WARS

FULL-LENGTH VERSION
BY JAMES McLURE

★

DRAMATISTS
PLAY SERVICE
INC.

PVT. WARS was presented by the McCarter Theatre (Nagle Jackson, Artistic Director; John Herochik, Managing Director) in Princeton, New Jersey, on July 20, 1989. The play was directed by Nagle Jackson; the lighting design was by Stephen J. Howe; the costume design was by Suzanne Elder; the stage manager was C. Townsend Olcott II; and the production manager was David York. The cast was as follows:

GATELY .... Kevin Chamberlin
NATWICK .... William Richert
SILVIO .... Robin Tate

PVT. WARS was first presented by Century Park Productions (Daniel Verdin, Executive Producer; Steven Markus and Sanford Jensen, Producers) at The Zephyr Theatre in Los Angeles, California, on August 30, 1984. The play was directed by John C. Fletcher; the set design was by "Jack" Fletcher; the lighting design was by Greg Sullivan; and the production stage manager was Alma Negro. The cast was as follows:

GATELY .... Gregory Grove
NATWICK .... Jeffery Combs
SILVIO .... Tony Campisi

A NOTE FROM THE DIRECTOR

This is a play about three Vietnam veterans waging their own private wars in a veterans' hospital. The Vietnam war ignited conflicts and emotional disturbance for many, if not most, of the thinking citizens of the United States. It caused a painful and necessary examination of conscience and it could be argued that our society is healthier for it. In this play — which is more of a comedy than anything else, a dark comedy to be sure — the conflicts and questioning seem to be wonderfully trivial, the minutiae of institutional life. As the play progresses we begin to learn the terrible truths which underlie the pranks and bickering. It is a microcosm which, in the classical mode of good theater, reflects the macrocosm of a society looking to be healed. Over and over the characters repeat the motto of the hospital: "You can leave anytime you want." More and more, that escape seems to be impossible. One's private wars must be resolved first.

The play had an instant success in its first production on Broadway in 1977 where it was performed as a one-act. Its new, expanded version has just premiered in Los Angeles. This McCarter production marked the European debut of this work when the company presented it in Oslo, Norway this past April.

Nagle Jackson

CHARACTERS

WOODRUFF GATELY—a young southerner. Childlike, mentally slow but not stupid. The kind of man who at age 30 might chase a fire engine to see where it was going.

SILVIO—Italian American. Street-wise, tough but not cruel.

NATWICK—a young man from Long Island. Intelligent, spoiled. He should never have been in the armed forces.

TIME

The 1970's.

SETTING

The lounge area of a veteran's hospital.

In the McCarter Theater production the transition speeches were tape recorded.

Pvt. Wars

ACT ONE

Breathing.
Blackness.
The sound of wind.
Cold, desperate.
This fades into sound of human breathing.
First breathing masculine, passionate as if making love.
It recedes.
Second breathing comes in louder than first breathing.
Second breathing is irregular, gasping, as if hyperventilating.
This breathing recedes, blends with first.
Third breathing, short, raspy, desperate tones, panic.
The breathings blend.
The three continue.
The wind sounds return.

THE RADIO

A sunny day. Gately at the table fixing a radio. Pause.
Silvio enters hurriedly. Pause. He notices Gately.

SILVIO. What the hell you doing?

GATELY. Fixing a radio.

SILVIO. What the hell for?

GATELY. It's for Hinson.

SILVIO. What's Hinson need a radio for? I need a radio more than Hinson.

GATELY. Why?

SILVIO. Hinson doesn't have any arms or legs.

GATELY. Yes, but you move around too much. This has to be plugged in.

SILVIO. I'll get an extension cord.

GATELY. I don't think that's such a great idea. You need something with batteries, transistors.

SILVIO. I got one of those.

GATELY. That's good.

SILVIO. One thing I've noticed about you, you concentrate and you do things slowly. How do you account for this?

GATELY. Hard drugs.

SILVIO. I see.

GATELY. It's for my nerves.

SILVIO. Do the drugs help?

GATELY. Oh yes. I hardly have any nerves left at all. (*Pause.*) Could you hand me that piece of wire? I want to do a good job on this. I figure if I do a good job of this radio, they may let me out of here.

SILVIO. You can get out any time you want.

GATELY. I know that.

SILVIO. But you figure if you finish that radio, they'll let you out.

GATELY. Sure. It's all part of the Free Enterprise system.

SILVIO. I see. (*Silvio refers to a pocket notebook.*) OK, I gotta go.

GATELY. OK.

SILVIO. Yeah, there's some orderly over in C Ward givin' those guys a lotta shit. Can you believe that? So — I gotta go.

GATELY. *OK.*

SILVIO. So, uh, you here a lot? You hang out here?

GATELY. Yeah.

SILVIO. You're . . . uh, Gately, right?

GATELY. Yeah.

SILVIO. Tell you what. I'll see you later. (*Silvio exits. Gately watches him go.*)

BLACKOUT

I DON'T WANT TO TALK ABOUT IT

> *Gately fixing radio. Natwick enters in robe and slippers, carrying a newspaper. He is visibly upset. He sits, opens paper, covering his face. He lowers paper.*

NATWICK. I don't want to talk about it.

GATELY. What?

NATWICK. I don't want to talk about it.

GATELY. What don't you want to talk about.

NATWICK. Look! What did I just say? What did I *just* say? I said I did not want to talk about it! OK?

GATELY. OK.

NATWICK. OK?

GATELY. OK.

NATWICK. Thank you. (*Gately whistles first verse of "Zippidy doo dah." Then sings, "Mr. Bluebird on my shoulder . . ."**) Oh, now come on! Do you mind? I'm trying to read.

GATELY. Natwick, if you won't tell me what not to talk about, how do you know I might not accidently start talking about it?

NATWICK. I wouldn't worry about it if I were you, the odds are ten trillion to one against it.

*See special note on copyright page.

8

GATELY. Oh.

NATWICK. (*Darkly.*) But I don't even want to take that chance.

GATELY. I'll bet I could guess what it is.

NATWICK. (*Amused.*) Don't even waste your time. (*Slight pause.*)

GATELY. Is it something that just happened to you?

NATWICK. (*Guarding.*) What?

GATELY. Did someone do something to you?

NATWICK. (*Sinking.*) I don't want —

GATELY. Was it staff?

NATWICK. Oh, all right! One down, two to go.

GATELY. Was it someone in the ward?

NATWICK. Two down, one to go.

GATELY. Was it Gleason?

NATWICK. (*Exulting.*) Three down, none to —

GATELY. Was it Silvio?

NATWICK. What?

GATELY. Was it Silvio? (*Silvio enters with a smile to suggest he has eaten Natwick's firstborn.*)

SILVIO. Hello, Gately.

GATELY. Hello, Silvio.

NATWICK. Hello, Silvio.

SILVIO. Hello, Natwick.

BLACKOUT

UNDERWEAR

Gately fixing radio. Silvio standing looking off intently, into the distance.

SILVIO. Would you look at that? Would you look at that? (*Pause.*) Hey, beautiful! Hey, gorgeous! Turn around! Ta-dah! (*Silvio unties his robe, flashes, reties robe. Smiles contentedly. Silvio slips underwear on underneath robe.*) My sister sent me these.

GATELY. Very nice.

SILVIO. It's good material. Care for a feel?

GATELY. Uh, not right now.

9

SILVIO. I don't know, I like the floppy kind of underwear. It gives you more of a sense of freedom, you know? You can flop around. One has mobility. (*Pause.*)

GATELY. That's very good. You could go on TV and advertise floppy underwear.

SILVIO. Yeah, I could if I wanted to y'know. Ain't got the time though. But I could if I wanted to y'know. Cause I believe in floppy underwear. Only one drawback to floppy underwear.

GATELY. What's that?

SILVIO. They make you feel like an old man. That's the trouble with life, Gately. You may find something you like, but if it makes you feel like an old man — what's the point? (*Pause.*) You know another thing makes you feel like an old man?

GATELY. An old woman?

SILVIO. Garters.

GATELY. You're right.

SILVIO. You damn right I'm right. I had to wear garters to my brother's wedding.

GATELY. Did it make you feel like an old man?

SILVIO. You damn right. Besides, the garters didn't work.

GATELY. Maybe you were wearing the wrong kinda socks.

SILVIO. Maybe you're right.

GATELY. What kind did you wear?

SILVIO. Athletic socks.

GATELY. You wore athletic socks to your brother's wedding?

SILVIO. You see, Gately, I'm Catholic.

GATELY. Did the Pope make you do it?

SILVIO. Don't get cute, Gately. It was his second marriage. OK? First time around I wear black socks. Second time around I figured, fuck it. You see, Gately, I respect the state of holy matrimony. And I respect the Holy Catholic Church.

GATELY. So do I . . . think you'll ever get married, Silvio?

SILVIO. Are you fuckin' kidding me? Let some bitch take all my money?

GATELY. I didn't know you had any money, Silvio.

SILVIO. What's that got to do with it?

GATELY. Well . . .

SILVIO. I just don't see what that's got to do with it. (*Pause.*) But, if I did meet the right girl, I'd marry her inna shot.

GATELY. Me too.

SILVIO. Cause I respect the State of Holy Matrimony.

GATELY. So do I.

SILVIO. I know you do. Let's shake on it. (*They stand and shake on it.*) Now, I'd like to return for a minute, if I may, to the subject of underwear.

GATELY. All right.

SILVIO. Now then. Floppy versus tight. Me? I don't see any comparison. Cause, I mean, in terms of underwear, what is a man looking for?

GATELY. Fashion?

SILVIO. Certainly fashion. I mean, you're with a chick, right? You don't want to take off your pants, right?—and have her laugh at your underwear?

GATELY. She might though, if you're wearing floppy underwear.

SILVIO. That's why you gotta get a good pattern. Take a look at these. Are these smart or what?

GATELY. They're pretty smart.

SILVIO. My sister sent me these.

GATELY. Your sister's got good taste in men's underwear.

SILVIO. Of course.

GATELY. Kinda makes you wonder, though.

SILVIO. What?

GATELY. How your sister got such good taste in men's underwear. •

SILVIO. (*Pointing finger.*) Hey. Watch it. (*Pause.*) OK. So the way I see it, a guy needs fashion and a guy needs mobility. And outside of that, there's nothing else a guy needs.

GATELY. Snugness.

SILVIO. Uh oh. I think I hear the voice of a tight underwear man here.

GATELY. Well, a guy doesn't always want floppy underwear.

SILVIO. Now wait a minute.

GATELY. Underwear are like socks.

SILVIO. Stop. I don't know if I can let that get by.

GATELY. You don't want your socks slipping down. A man wants snug socks.

SILVIO. (*Pondering.*) Socks are like underwear. (*Pause.*) What kind are you wearing?

GATELY. Black ones.

SILVIO. (*Troubled.*) Oh yeah?

GATELY. Yeah.

SILVIO. Are they tight?

GATELY. (*Underneath table, wiggles his foot.*) They're pretty tight.

SILVIO. They're not black silk, are they?

GATELY. Black polyester, I think. But all mine got holes in them.

SILVIO. Of course they've got holes. It's a modern convenience.

GATELY. I've got holes on the balls.

SILVIO. Holes on the balls!

GATELY. I've got to get some new ones.

SILVIO. I guess so.

GATELY. But, I've got a problem. I got different sizes. My left is bigger than my right.

SILVIO. Well, how much difference can there be?

GATELY. About an inch. One's about nine inches long.

SILVIO. What?!

GATELY. The other's about 10 inches.

SILVIO. Nine and ten inches?

GATELY. I was born that way.

SILVIO. Jesus Christ. What about . . . you know . . . Mr. In-Between?

GATELY. What?

SILVIO. Never mind. (*Pause.*)

GATELY. I find though, if I buy, oh nine to say eleven, that fits everything.

SILVIO. You are not talking about around are you?

GATELY. Hell no! I'm talking about length. What's the matter, Silvio?

SILVIO. I don't want to talk about it. (*Silvio sinks into darkest depression. Natwick enters. Sits.*)

GATELY. Hello, Natwick.

NATWICK. I don't want to talk about it. (*Pause. Notices*

12

Silvio's depression.) What's the matter with Little Mary Sunshine?

GATELY. He doesn't want to talk about it.

NATWICK. Very intelligent of him.

GATELY. Pretty soon I'll be talking to myself around here. Say, Natwick. What size feet do you have?

NATWICK. About a nine, ten.

GATELY. Can I borrow some socks? Mine are wearing out on the balls of my feet.

NATWICK. Do you still have athlete's foot?

SILVIO. Wait, wait, wait, wait, wait, wait, wait, what?

NATWICK. Does he still have athlete's foot?

SILVIO. You were talking about the balls of your feet.

GATELY. Of course.

SILVIO. Oh, you were talking about socks!

GATELY. Yes.

SILVIO. Oh. You hear that, Natwick? He was talking about socks.

NATWICK. Yes, I'm overwhelmed.

SILVIO. Oh. Wow. Great. That's great. That's terrific. Jesus, that's beautiful. Yeah for the socks. (*Exits, relieved.*)

NATWICK. What did you say about socks?

GATELY. I don't know. (*They look off to where Silvio has exited. Gately returns to radio. Natwick reads paper.*)

BLACKOUT

FREE ENTERPRISE

Silvio and Gately at table. A great deal of tension.

GATELY. Wire. (*Silvio hands him a piece of wire.*) Screwdriver. (*Silvio hands it to him.*) Do-hickey. (*Silvio looks puzzled. Hands him a radio.*) No, that's a doomaflatchie. I need a do-hickey. (*Silvio picks up another part. Gately inspects part. Puts it aside wearily.*) That's a thingamabob. I need a do-hickey. (*Silvio makes a "calm down" gesture, searches through the pile of parts very meticulously. Finds a part, holds it up for Gately's approval. Gately frowns. Silvio shakes his head. Gately shakes his head. Silvio selects new part. Gately takes it, eyes it cautiously, then smiles sagely. Returns to work. Stops.*) All you gotta do is get from point A to point B.

SILVIO. Point A to point B.

GATELY. (*Conspiratorially.*) Point A is where you are. Point B is where you're going. (*He demonstrates with radio parts.*) Point A . . . Point B.

SILVIO. Free enterprise?

GATELY. Free enterprise.

SILVIO. I see.

GATELY. It's simple, really.

SILVIO. I see.

GATELY. You gotta keep things rolling, keep things moving.

SILVIO. Are things rolling?

GATELY. Hell, no.

SILVIO. Then does free enterprise work?

GATELY. Hell, yes. See, I'm working on this radio. And it's not just helping me. It's helping Hinson . . . Free enterprise . . . helps . . . everybody.

SILVIO. Like therapy.

GATELY. (*Impatiently.*) Noooo. Not like therapy. Therapy doesn't help anybody.

SILVIO. What about the guy over in "D" ward that's fixing a radio.

GATELY. (*Taking in the enormity of this.*) There's a what? (*Terror.*) No—

SILVIO. Hey, look I was just kiddin'.

GATELY. . . . you were.

SILVIO. Yeah, there ain't no guy over there.

GATELY. (*Unsure.*) Yeah, there ain't no guy over there.

SILVIO. Hey, just a little joke.

GATELY. Yeah. (*Chuckling. Stops chuckling. They both chuckle. Stop. Works. Stops work. Disturbed.*) See this radio is for Hinson.

SILVIO. Hinson doesn't know what a radio is. Hinson is a drool.

GATELY. No . . . he knows, he knows.

SILVIO. So you fix the radio.

GATELY. I'm rollin'. I'm outta here. And I won't be back.

14

SILVIO. Maybe they *bring* you back.

GATELY. No. They won't be able to find me.

SILVIO. Oh, they'll find you.

GATELY. Who'll find me?

SILVIO. Federal marshals . . . cops . . . drug enforcement agents . . . professional musicians . . . (*Pause. Gately strikes free enterprise.*)

GATELY. "If one guy like me can make a radio work — then America works."

SILVIO. You gonna do this all by yourself?

GATELY. Yes . . . professional musicians.

SILVIO. Yes.

GATELY. . . . I'm going for the big stuff.

SILVIO. You're goin' for the bucks.

GATELY. For even bigger than that.

SILVIO. What's bigger than the bucks?

GATELY. . . . I'm gonna be free.

SILVIO. Gately, I wish you luck. Gately! Look at that squirrel. (*Gately returns to work. Can't find part. Doubts his sanity.*)

BLACKOUT

HINSON'S DEAD

Gately and Natwick.

NATWICK. Why are you still fixing that radio?

GATELY. For Hinson.

NATWICK. Hinson's dead.

GATELY. What?

NATWICK. Hinson's dead.

GATELY. How can he be dead? I saw him just yesterday.

NATWICK. He died last night.

GATELY. He was perfectly all right. He didn't have any arms or legs, but he was all right.

NATWICK. Gately, he died last night.

GATELY. One day he's alive, the next he's dead.

NATWICK. That's life. (*Pause.*)

GATELY. But this is a hospital.

NATWICK. That's the way it is in a hospital. Either you get better or you die or you rot. (*Gately, stunned, gets up, walks away from table. Turns. Looks at radio.*) Look at it this way. At least you don't have to waste your time on that stupid radio. Gately, we all die sooner or later. You know, Gately, in many ways we're alike.

GATELY. We're nothing alike.

NATWICK. Of course we are. We're both intelligent and sensitive.

GATELY. Am I?

NATWICK. Well, you're sensitive.

GATELY. Am I?

NATWICK. You'd have to be either sensitive or just plain stupid to fix a radio for Hinson.

GATELY. Why?

NATWICK. Everyone knew Hinson was going to die. So do you want to play chess? Gately, what are you doing?

GATELY. Fixing the radio.

NATWICK. Gately, Hinson's dead.

GATELY. I know that.

NATWICK. Gately, don't be a fool.

GATELY. Someone else can use it.

NATWICK. You're deluding yourself.

GATELY. No, I'm not. If I fix this radio, they'll let me out of here.

NATWICK. You can get out anytime you want to.

GATELY. You see, Natwick, every cloud has a silver lining.

NATWICK. Yes. But that's just what it is.

GATELY. What?

NATWICK. A lining. You take out that lining, you know what you've got?

GATELY. What?

NATWICK. A cloud. A very dark, dangerous cloud.

SILVIO. (*Entering.*) Hello, Gately.

GATELY. Hello, Silvio.

SILVIO. Natwick, go fuck yourself. (*Natwick gapes and exits.*) the thing about Natwick — you tell him to do something and by God, he goes and does it. (*Gately returns to radio. Silvio seated.*) Gately, I've been thinking of buying a kilt.

GATELY. A Kilt?

16

SILVIO. Yeah, it's a kind of dress that guys in Scotland wear. (*Pause.*) It's kinda like a cheerleader's skirt.

GATELY. If you want a cheerleader's skirt, why don't you just buy a cheerleader's skirt?

SILVIO. I don't want no cheerleader's skirt.

GATELY. Oh.

SILVIO. What would I do with a cheerleader's skirt?

GATELY. I have no idea.

SILVIO. Hey wait a minute. You think I want to wear a girl's skirt? You think that? Is that what you think?

GATELY. Look, I don't care —

SILVIO. Look, I don't care that you don't care. Who cares!

GATELY. Not me.

SILVIO. Look, I don't want to wear a dress, OK?

GATELY. OK.

SILVIO. I want to wear a kilt. (*Pause.*) Look, I read somewhere that Scots have a very high potency rate. So I said to myself, what have they got that we haven't got?

GATELY. Kilts?

SILVIO. Right. Gately, did you know tight pants weaken the sperm count.

GATELY. They prove that?

SILVIO. They've practically proved that. Science doesn't have time to bullshit. Gately, what happens in the Spring?

GATELY. Flowers?

SILVIO. That's right. Nature starts rejuvenating itself. Gately, picture if you will, an Oregon stream in the spring of the year, the icy waters teaming with salmon. Indians poised, ready to spear them as they spawn. Returning from the sea to a very old place. Now, these salmon returning to spawn are called grilse. The grilse overcome incredible obstacles in order to spawn. They have to fight their way past dams and rocks and Indians and kids with dynamite sticks.

GATELY. Are we still talking about the sperm count?

SILVIO. Gately, I want you to think of your sperm as a salmon.

GATELY. OK.

SILVIO. Think of your sperm as grilse.

GATELY. Grilse!

SILVIO. The sperm is fighting it's way up the vagina!

17

Thrashing on to the spawning grounds! Over rocks and dams and Indians.

GATELY. In the vagina?

SILVIO. But the weak sperm can't make it!

GATELY. They give out.

SILVIO. They poop out. So the sperm pulls over to the side of the vagina. Worse thing they could possibly do!

GATELY. Poor little guys.

SILVIO. In the end all the salmon die. They spawn and they die. And except for the one sperm, and I'm talking millions here, Gately, except for the one sperm that fertilizes the egg, this is also the fate of the sperm. See, all the sperms are there supporting the other sperm. It's the buddy system. And one guy gets through. One guy. Think about it. (*They both stare out at the world, impressed by the majesty of Silvio's speech.*)

GATELY. Have you ever read Hiawatha?

SILVIO. No.

GATELY. It's full of rocks and rivers and Indians. Do the sperm have a leader?

SILVIO. Well, science isn't sure, Gately. I think they take turns.

GATELY. (*Pause.*) Do you think the sperm know they're gonna die?

SILVIO. At present, Gately, science doesn't know how much the sperm knows. But we can say this about the sperm. (*Thinks.*) It has a helluva sense of direction. (*They both look out.*)

BLACKOUT

SUPERIOR

Natwick and Gately playing a game of chess. Gately pondering a move.

NATWICK. You know, if we were playing professionally your time would be up.

GATELY. Oh. Are you a professional, Natwick? (*Cockily.*) Is that what you are—a pro? Heh, heh, heh. I gotcha where I

18

want you now. (*Gately makes a move.*) I like this better'n checkers.

NATWICK. (*Moving*) Checkmate.

GATELY. What?

NATWICK. Checkmate. (*Knocking over his piece.*) Checkmate. (*Pause.*) Do you wanna play again?

GATELY. No.

NATWICK. There's only one way to improve your game.

GATELY. Yeah — don't play.

NATWICK. (*Singing.*) "Zippidy-Doo-Dah. Zippidy-Aye . . ." "Mr. Bluebird's on my shoulder."* (*Natwick sings this about five times.*)

GATELY. Do you mind? I'm trying to work here.

NATWICK. You're patronizing me.

GATELY. I wouldn't patronize you.

NATWICK. (*Patronizingly.*) You probably don't even know what "patronizingly" means.

GATELY. Natwick, why do you act so superior?

NATWICK. I don't act superior. I am superior.

GATELY. You're not necessarily superior. I'll tell you something. Silvio's been working on this theory. If you wear kilts your sperm will be more like a grilse's.

NATWICK. What?

GATELY. Grilse are the salmon that fight their way upstream.

NATWICK. No.

GATELY. What?

NATWICK. Grilse are the salmon that fight their way downstream. Grilse are the young salmon, not the mature salmon.

GATELY. What do you call mature salmon?

NATWICK. Salmon.

GATELY. What about kilts? Silvio says we should wear kilts to make us more potent.

NATWICK. Silvio wants to dress like a pervert.

GATELY. Why?

NATWICK. Because he is a pervert. And if we ran around in

*See special note on copyright page.

19

kilts, we'd be just as perverted as he is.

GATELY. What about the Scots? They run around in kilts. What about them?

NATWICK. They're perverted.

GATELY. Have you ever read "Hiawatha"?

BLACKOUT

HUMANOIDS

Natwick reading from note cards.

NATWICK. Hello there! This is your Entertainment Director, Pfc. Natwick. Tonight's movie is *Humanoids from the Deep*, starring Vic Morrow. (*We hear "boos."*) OK. You think it's easy getting quality movies on my budget? (*More "boos."*) It's all about these underwater vegetable monsters who eat people. (*More "boos."*) And I quote: "Monsters with a penchant for beachgoers. Contains nudity, rape, and other scenes of sexual violence." (*They cheer.*) Great. You guys *like* this one already and last week you *hated A Star is Born.* You guys are sick.

BLACKOUT

TRANSITION

PSYCHIATRIST. Silvio, I want you to relax.

SILVIO. Doc, I'm relaxed.

PSYCHIATRIST. I'm here to help you. Now just relax.

SILVIO. I am relaxed.

PSYCHIATRIST. Silvio.

SILVIO. What?

PSYCHIATRIST. If you really relaxed, you'd put down the lamp and get off my desk.

20

SILVIO'S MONOLOGUE

SILVIO. I don't know. I have these strange thoughts. They're not violent. (*Pause.*) Some of them are violent. The other day I, uhm, was talking to this old woman. And she was talking and I just wanted to do some outrageous thing to her. Like slap her. Or pull her false teeth out. Or play with the flab on her face. I mean, I wouldn't but — it's something I think about. (*Pause.*) When I was little I used to think I could talk to God. In fact, I thought I could talk to God better than anybody in the world and I didn't understand why world leaders didn't come to me to pray to God to solve the world's problems. I'd sit in church with my family. And my mother — my mother is a very beautiful woman. She looks like Italian women on jars of spaghetti sauce. And she's got big old bosoms. And I like 'em. And I don't care what that sounds like 'cause it's one of my favorite parts of my mother. (*Pause.*) And I remember when my father died, it, uh, she showed great dignity. She took my hand and she said, "You go take care of your sister now." And I said, "Who's gonna take care of you?" And she said, "I can take care of myself, you take care of your sister." And I said, "But I want to take care of you?" And she said, "Look, you get in there and take care of your sister before I knock you into the middle of next week." And I did. And my sister was so pretty when she — was in her confirmation dress. (*Pause.*) Somebody's been flashing the nurses? I don't know anything about that. It wasn't me. (*Pause.*) It wasn't me.

BLACKOUT

HEMINGWAY/PEACHES

NATWICK. The New York *Times* review of books.
GATELY. What?
NATWICK. I don't want to talk about it . . . can't they write about anyone else?

21

GATELY. What?

NATWICK. I don't want to talk about it . . . I mean the man was not a decent individual.

GATELY. He wasn't?

NATWICK. No! He made fun of F. Scott Fitzgerald's penis, for God's sake.

GATELY. He did? That's awful. What did F. Scott say?

NATWICK. Oh. You know. The usual.

GATELY. The usual?

NATWICK. Well, y'know. It's not what he *said*. It's the way he said it.

GATELY. Hmmm.

NATWICK. And they keep writing *books* about him.

GATELY. About who?

NATWICK. About Hemingway! Another book on Hemingway!

GATELY. Hmmm.

NATWICK. I mean, or, he was a great writer. But! Why did he take his own life?

GATELY. Why?

NATWICK. I don't want to talk about it . . . of course, don't forget he was no longer the man he once was.

GATELY. Who is for Christ's sake?

NATWICK. I tell you, Gately, if I had any kind of courage at all, I'd go straight to my room, take out a razor and slash my wrists. Oh God, I wish I could.

GATELY. What's preventing you?

NATWICK. I use an electric.

GATELY. I'll lend you one of mine.

NATWICK. What kind of thing is that to say to a person?

GATELY. Well, if you really wanted to.

NATWICK. I don't really want to.

GATELY. You don't?

NATWICK. No. Suicide is a plea for help.

GATELY. Well, I'm trying to help. I'll lend you the razor blade.

NATWICK. That's just great. A man reaches out to his fellow man, a hand reaches out into the darkness for a little comfort, a little compassion, I reach out to you—and you hand me a razor blade.

GATELY. Okay. I won't lend you the razor blade.

NATWICK. What's the matter? Don't you trust me?

GATELY. Yes.

NATWICK. You'll get it back.

GATELY. How? You'll be dead. You'll be stretched out on the floor —

NATWICK. Actually, a bath tub.

GATELY. Bath tub?

NATWICK. Gately, for instance, suppose I can't cope with the world when they let me out of here.

GATELY. You can get out any time you want to.

NATWICK. I know that. I see my suicide, Gately, as a beautiful thing. There I am in my mother's home, my wrists slashed, my blood filling the bath tub.

GATELY. But why a bath tub?

NATWICK. I don't want to make a mess.

GATELY. Why?

NATWICK. My mother would kill me.

GATELY. You'll be dead. She can't do anything to you then.

NATWICK. You don't know my mother. (*Pause.*) You know, you don't know what it's like growing up rich.

GATELY. You know — you're right.

NATWICK. When you're rich there's only one way to go — down.

GATELY. Same thing when you're poor. Only it's a different direction.

NATWICK. All my life, I've known I was going to fail. My mother had a brilliant career planned for me. Anything less than Secretary of State would have been considered a failure. I remember my childhood as a succession of summer homes moving further and further out on Long Island. My sense of failure grew in proportion to the size of the houses, each one larger than the last. When we got the place at Montauk, I joined the Army. Everyone was surprised that the Army took me. Including me.

GATELY. Isn't it funny how some days we can shoot the breeze like this and other days, we just can't talk at all. Isn't that funny? Why is that, you think? Huh? What do you think?

NATWICK. Inertia.

GATELY. In what?

NATWICK. The state of inertia, the lack of momentum, the inability to move. . . .

GATELY. Oh, yeah.

NATWICK. There are good days and there are bad days. On good days, I can talk. On bad days — well, one dares not eat a peach, as they say.

GATELY. Eat a peach. Why wouldn't a person dare eat a peach?

NATWICK. It's something someone once said.

GATELY. Who said it?

NATWICK. T.S. Eliot.

GATELY. T.S. Eliot was afraid to eat a peach?

NATWICK. Gately.

GATELY. Was he allergic to them?

NATWICK. Prufrock didn't dare to eat a peach.

GATELY. Was Prufrock allergic to them?

NATWICK. Prufrock is not a person. He's a poem.

GATELY. I know that. (*Pause.*) Why wouldn't he dare to eat a peach?

NATWICK. Because he was afraid.

GATELY. Was there something wrong with the peach? Had the peach gone bad?

NATWICK. There was nothing wrong with the peach.

GATELY. What was he afraid of then?

NATWICK. Life.

GATELY. Life?

NATWICK. Yes.

GATELY. He was so afraid of life that he couldn't eat a peach? That's disgraceful!

NATWICK. It was the small things in life that defeated him. The momentary terrors.

GATELY. Like what?

NATWICK. Old age. Old women. Tea parties.

GATELY. Tea parties! Old women! Hell, that's just minor league stuff! I hope this Prufrock never runs into any of the MAJOR PROBLEMS OF LIFE. Then he really wouldn't be able to eat the peach!

NATWICK. Why are you getting so upset?

GATELY. Who's upset! I don't even know the guy!

Prufrock's *your* friend, not mine. Where'd he eat this peach?

NATWICK. On a beach.

GATELY. Well, that's just dandy. The guy's so sensitive he can't eat a goddamn peach on a goddamn beach.

NATWICK. It's just a metaphor, Gately, OK?

GATELY. I just hope this guy never gets drafted, that's all I hope.

NATWICK. The guy can't get drafted. The guy's in a poem, Gately, you know what poems are?

GATELY. I read poems.

NATWICK. When?

GATELY. All the time! I read 'em till I'm sick of 'em.

NATWICK. What poems? Give me one.

GATELY. "Hiawatha." It's a great poem! Look it up!

NATWICK. Well, it's like that.

GATELY. What is?

NATWICK. You can't draft Hiawatha.

GATELY. Even if you did, what makes you think he'd serve? Hiawatha was one of the greatest Indians of all time. What makes you think he'd fight for this shitty Army? He'd go to Canada first.

NATWICK. Are you saying Hiawatha was a draft dodger?

GATELY. Not if it was an Indian war. If it was an Indian war, hell, he'd put on his war paint, get in his canoe and go whip ass.

NATWICK. (*Weary.*) But only his own wars.

GATELY. That's right! And if everybody would fight their own private wars, things would be all right. But no, people have to stick their noses into other people's wars! You see what I mean, Natwick? You see what I'm trying to say?

NATWICK. No.

GATELY. The thing about the world is . . . the thing about the world is . . . the world is . . . you see what I'm trying to say?

NATWICK. And that's why I don't want to talk about it.

GATELY. (*Pause.*) You just can't stand to lose an argument. Can you?

NATWICK. Who says I lost? Who says I lost?

GATELY. Oh, you lost.

NATWICK. I certainly did not. I do not lose arguments. I

25

especially do not lose arguments to you.

GATELY. I whipped your ass.

NATWICK. You whipped nothing.

GATELY. Whipped it.

NATWICK. You are a hillbilly. (*Natwick exiting.*)

GATELY. (*Shouting.*) Mr. Inertia! (*Gately returns to fixing radio. Off-stage we hear Silvio's voice.*)

SILVIO. Hey, gorgeous. Turn around. Ta-dah! Woo! (*Entering.*) Be honest, c'mon. Don't hold back. Say what you gotta say. You *know* what you want to know.

GATELY. What?

SILVIO. Did you ever ask yourself the secret of my incredible sexual power over women?

GATELY. No.

SILVIO. Why the nurses can't resist me?

GATELY. The nurses hate you, Silvio.

SILVIO. Ah. That's what they would have you believe.

GATELY. They got me believin' it.

SILVIO. You wanna hear a great line for picking girls up?

GATELY. Sure.

SILVIO. Now this works best for Catholic girls.

GATELY. OK.

SILVIO. You tell 'em you're a priest.

GATELY. A priest.

SILVIO. OK. Look, we'll set the scene. This is what they call settin' the scene. Now you're sitting there. At the table. What can this table be?

GATELY. A table.

SILVIO. OK. We'll make it a table. We're in a night club.

GATELY. Can it be a single's joint?

SILVIO. Gately, you been to a single joint?

GATELY. No.

SILVIO. OK, I tell you what. In settin' the scene we'll make this a single's joint.

GATELY. (*Awed.*) Where'd you learn all this?

SILVIO. Once I hung around a USO group that was rehearsing. A Bob Hope thing. I tell you somethin', Gately . . .

GATELY. Yeah.

SILVIO. Never be afraid to mingle in the arts.

GATELY. All right.

SILVIO. OK, so we're in a single's joint. And you're a broad. Everybody's being hustled. It's a fucking meat market!

GATELY. What's a nice girl like me doing in a place like this?

SILVIO. That's it! That's it! That's what's called gettin' into character!

GATELY. Am I lonely?

SILVIO. Are you lonely? A face like that. What do you think?

GATELY. I'm lonely, huh?

SILVIO. That's right. You're like ugly Catholic girls all over the world. You're like a different breed. You sit there being ugly, ruining life for everybody else.

GATELY. Are you lonely?

SILVIO. Gately! I'm a priest! Of course I'm lonely. I'm one of the loneliest, horniest guys on the face of the earth. OK, you're sitting there by yourself. So I come in; and I'm very depressed, and I'm very mysterious. So I come in.

GATELY. Hey! Look! It's a priest!

SILVIO. What are you doing?

GATELY. I'm saying hello.

SILVIO. Gately, you don't know I'm a priest.

GATELY. But aren't you wearing a priest shirt?

SILVIO. No. I'm being casual.

GATELY. But don't you have your thing on?

SILVIO. My thing?

GATELY. The collar thing.

SILVIO. No.

GATELY. But you're being mysterious?

SILVIO. Very.

GATELY. Are you being scary?

SILVIO. Gately, I don't want to *scare* them. I'm being mysterious.

GATELY. Like Dracula?

SILVIO. Gately, you don't listen to me anymore, Gately. That worries me, Gately. Now, we're gonna do it again. You're sitting there by yourself. You're lonely. OK, so I come in. And I'm very depressed. So I come in and I look around. No, you don't see me yet, Gately. I see you. I come

27

over and I say, "Pardon me, miss, is this seat taken?"

GATELY. Yes, it is.

SILVIO. What?

GATELY. Buzz off.

SILVIO. No. You don't say nothing.

GATELY. You want me to call the management?

SILVIO. That's not the way it goes.

GATELY. Male chauvinist pig.

SILVIO. Gately.

GATELY. What?

SILVIO. Don't give me such a hard time, OK?

GATELY. I just want to make it realistic.

SILVIO. OK. But you're making it too realistic. We'll do it again. So you're sitting there by yourself, lonely. I come in very depressed. So I come in. I'm looking around. I'm checking things out. You don't see me yet, Gately—I see you and I come over and I say, "Pardon me, miss, but is this seat taken?"

GATELY. Well, why not.

SILVIO. Mind if I sit down?

GATELY. Well, why not.

SILVIO. May I order you another drink?

GATELY. Well, sure.

SILVIO. Bartender. Two more of the same. Do you mind if I smoke?

GATELY. Well, why not. (*Silvio takes out two cigarettes, puts them in his mouth, lights them both. He offers her one.*) I don't want it.

SILVIO. Why not?

GATELY. You've slobbered all over it.

SILVIO. No, I haven't.

GATELY. You've had it in your mouth.

SILVIO. Gately, take the fuckin' cigarette. (*Gately takes the cigarette.*) I hope you won't think I'm being too personal but . . . what's your name?

GATELY. Woodruff Gately.

SILVIO. Woodruff?

GATELY. Woodruff.

SILVIO. I've never known a girl named Woodruff before.

GATELY. You've never known a girl like me.

SILVIO. If I seem a little nervous, it's because I don't usually come to this kind of place. Have you ever come to this kind of place?

GATELY. I'm a Baptist.

SILVIO. You must be very lonely.

GATELY. Why, because I'm a Baptist?

SILVIO. (*Putting his hand on Gately's leg.*) Can I tell you something very personal?

GATELY. OK, but don't get smutty.

SILVIO. I just wanted to tell you that I don't get much of a chance to meet beautiful women. You see, actually, I'm a priest.

GATELY. Well, I don't get much of a chance to meet men. You see, actually, I'm a lesbian.

SILVIO. (*Angrily.*) That's it! Forget it, Gately.

GATELY. I'm sorry.

SILVIO. No! No! Let's just forget it. I try to teach you something! Give you the benefit of my experience, my life! You know what you are? I'll tell you what you are. A fucking ingrate, that's what you are. Why'd you make her a lesbian?

GATELY. I don't know.

SILVIO. Not even a priest could pick up a lesbian. Nobody could pick up a lesbian.

GATELY. A lesbian could!

SILVIO. Who cares! That does me no good. I can't become a lesbian every time I wanna get laid.

GATELY. No.

SILVIO. You see my point.

GATELY. You could become a transvestite.

SILVIO. What?

GATELY. Wear women's clothes.

SILVIO. But I don't want to wear women's clothes.

GATELY. I know you don't.

SILVIO. I know I don't, too.

GATELY. You want to wear a kilt.

SILVIO. That's right.

GATELY. Which is *nearly* women's clothes.

SILVIO. Don't you like women? (*Pause.*) Don't you? Don't you? This is a big fuckin' waste. I'll tell you something buddy, from now on, you're on your own. And I wish you luck

29

because at the rate you're going you may *never* get laid. (*He exits. Returns.*) Gately, I'm gonna get you laid.

GATELY. You are.

SILVIO. What kind of friend would *I* be if I didn't want *you* to get laid?

GATELY. I don't know.

SILVIO. Not much of a friend, Gately. We're gonna go out and we're not coming back till we get Gately laid.

GATELY. . . . Could be a long night.

BLACKOUT

DRESSING GATELY

Gately and Natwick. Gately in his underwear. Natwick with a pile of clothes on the table and chairs.

NATWICK. So you want to borrow my clothes.

GATELY. Just for tonight. Just for a date.

NATWICK. And you don't have a pass.

GATELY. No.

NATWICK. I don't approve of this, but here are the clothes. (*Pause. Gately inspects shoes.*) What about those shoes?

GATELY. They're a little faggoty looking.

NATWICK. They're two tones.

GATELY. We'll steer clear of those. Oh, I like these.

NATWICK. The wing tips?

GATELY. They look like they'll take off.

NATWICK. Those are not available.

GATELY. What?

NATWICK. Not all of these items are available. (*Pause.*)

GATELY. What would you suggest?

NATWICK. Given the short time I've had to consider this, I would suggest something along these lines. (*Natwick offers him clothes. Gately slips into them. It is a yachting coat and slacks, with cap.*) Why do you want these?

GATELY. Silvio and I are going to pick up girls.

NATWICK. . . . I don't want any stains.

GATELY. Huh?

30

NATWICK. Don't buy any drinks that will stain.
GATELY. What drinks stain?
NATWICK. Anything with Grenadine.
GATELY. OK. I won't buy anything with Grenadine . . . I don't know what it is anyway.
NATWICK. Well, is this satisfactory?
GATELY. Yes, it is.
NATWICK. That will be fifteen dollars.
GATELY. Fifteen dollars!!

BLACKOUT

NATWICK'S SUICIDE

Natwick comes in drunk, in bathrobe, tie.

NATWICK. Great. They've gone out on a date. They didn't even invite me. They're my best friends and even they hate me. They hate me. They hate me almost as much as I hate them. "I should have been a pair of ragged claws scuffling across the floors of silent seas." Say. That's good . . . (*Realization.*) Of course, it's good, asshole. That's T.S. Eliot. (*He pulls the tie very sharply around his neck. He ties the other end around the neck of chair. He tosses chair over. It jerks him over. Inspects tie / chair.*) Of course. This is the way to pull teeth, not kill yourself. Let's get serious. (*He gets up. He takes out a piece of paper. Reads.*) Isn't anything I write original? (*Reading from paper.*)
"I dare not meet your eyes in dreams.
For love is not the song it seems.
The breach between what seems and means
comes to us only in our dreams."
They'll appreciate me when I'm gone. (*He takes a bottle of pills from his pocket.*) Barbituates. There's the ticket. Good 'ol barbituates and alcohol. Great death. The death most often selected by celebrities. Sure. Won't feel a thing. (*He swallows the pills. Washes it down with alcohol.*) Won't be long now . . . soon will be dead . . . that's a depressing thought. Natwick. You are a loathsome individual. No, I'm

31

not. I am an invention of myself. A stillbirth who lived and gave birth to himself. And I lived. (*Pause.*) There's never anyone to dance with. (*He dances alone. Elegantly, gracefully.*)

BLACKOUT

STARS

Night. Silvio and Gately come staggering in.

SILVIO. Well, you blew it.
GATELY. Yeah.
SILVIO. I take you out and what happens?
GATELY. I blow it.
SILVIO. You talked to those girls alone.
GATELY. Yeah.
SILVIO. And it worked.
GATELY. Yeah.
SILVIO. You were alone with 'em for five minutes and they asked *us* to go home with *them*.
GATELY. Yeah.
SILVIO. What'd you tell those people?
GATELY. I don't know.
SILVIO. Then we get back to their place and they offer us booze and drugs. They want to get *us* drunk! What'd you tell those people?
GATELY. I don't know.
SILVIO. Then they say they have to change into something more comfortable and they come back in the Annette Funicello babydoll pajamas. What'd you *tell* those people?
GATELY. I talked to 'em like I talk to you.
SILVIO. You didn't see *me* change into the babydoll pajamas, did ya?
GATELY. No.
SILVIO. No. So then, you're in the bedroom with your chick. I'm on the sofa with my chick. And you and your chick come out and she says we have to leave because if she made it with you it'd spoil it for her for other men for the rest of her

life. And *my* chick went along with it. What'd you tell those people?

GATELY. I don't want to talk about it. (*Pause. Gately looks at the sky.*) Silvio.

SILVIO. Yeah, Gately.

GATELY. Where do we go when we die. (*No answer.*) What good is it to know about grilse and salmon and girls if we don't know where we go when we die?

SILVIO. I don't know.

GATELY. Where is Hinson now? . . . Up there.

SILVIO. I don't know. When you get there you can build him a radio . . . just never forget . . . you walked with kings.

GATELY. Yeah. Kings. (*They both inhale. Gately takes bottle from Silvio.*)

BLACKOUT

END ACT ONE

ACT TWO

RESTRICTED AREA

NATWICK. What're you doing here?
GATELY. What?
NATWICK. This is a restricted area.
GATELY. Well, what are *you* doing here then?
NATWICK. I have designated staff status.
GATELY. What?
NATWICK. I'm the designated Entertainment Director.
GATELY. Well, I'm here. No one uses this place. I found it.
NATWICK. (*Dragging up chair.*) Very well. We'll make this a designated shared space. (*Pause.*) Oh, by the way, I'm a totally independent individual. That's one item you need not fear or doubt. I need no one. I will never ask you for help.

BLACKOUT

THE CUP

Gately fixing a radio. Natwick enters in near panic.

NATWICK. Gately, you've got to help me.
GATELY. I'm busy.
NATWICK. Gately, this is a matter of life and death.
GATELY. I'm busy.
NATWICK. Gately, would you look at me! (*Natwick lifts hand from pocket secretively. He holds a cup in his hand. He lowers hand back into his pocket.*)
GATELY. Natwick, you've got a cup in your pocket.
NATWICK. Yes.
GATELY. Why do you have a cup in your pocket?
NATWICK. Actually, I've got a cup glued to my hand in my pocket.
GATELY. Why would you glue a cup to your hand?
NATWICK. You idiot!! I didn't do it! Silvio did it! He handed me a cup of coffee and suddenly I was glued. (*Gately tries, unsuccessfully, to disengage Natwick from cup.*)

34

GATELY. (*Fascinated.*) Let's see. He must have used that super epoxy glue. You know it dries in five seconds?

NATWICK. Yes, I know.

GATELY. I always wondered if this stuff would work.

NATWICK. Yes, well, it works.

GATELY. You better take that over to the shop. They have something that'll take that off.

NATWICK. What?

GATELY. An acid solution.

NATWICK. Acid.

GATELY. It might burn.

NATWICK. Yeah. Like molten lava might burn. I'm going to find an orderly —

GATELY. Why? You'll get Silvio in trouble.

NATWICK. I *want* to get Silvio in trouble.

GATELY. Natwick! You've got to understand. Silvio's wound has left him emotionally scarred.

NATWICK. You want emotional scars? I have a urine bag strapped to my side. You think that's fun? Going through life as a portable toilet?

GATELY. Silvio's wound is different.

NATWICK. I don't want to hear about Silvio's wound.

GATELY. Natwick.

NATWICK. I don't want to hear about Silvio's wound. I'm going to find an orderly.

GATELY. You do and Silvio'll kill you.

NATWICK. What kind of wound was it?

GATELY. Shrapnel.

NATWICK. Well. Shrapnel. That's not so bad.

GATELY. It blew off his testicles and his penis.

NATWICK. Wow. That explains a lot. Sure. He flashes the nurses to assert his lack of manhood.

GATELY. Sure! That explains the flashing!

NATWICK. It explains his macho act.

GATELY. Sure. It explains the macho act.

NATWICK. It explains everything.

GATELY. It even explains the cup.

NATWICK. No, it doesn't explain the cup.

GATELY. No. I guess he just hates your guts. And thinks you're a wussie, and a jerk, an asshole . . .

35

NATWICK. Yeah. That explains the cup.

GATELY. (*Pause.*) What're you gonna do?

NATWICK. I don't know I'm sorry. I refuse to feel pity for a man who glues my fingers together. Why do you think he hates me so much?

GATELY. You get on his nerves.

NATWICK. Yeah. But why?

GATELY. You read Tolstoy.

NATWICK. What?

GATELY. One day you said that no man can call himself cultured until he's read "War and Peace."

NATWICK. So.

GATELY. Silvio didn't get past the list of characters.

NATWICK. I don't want to talk about it.

GATELY. That's another thing. He doesn't like it when you won't talk about it.

NATWICK. Why?

GATELY. He says you're avoiding reality.

NATWICK. Of course I am.

GATELY. He says you're being secretive.

NATWICK. I'm not secretive. I'm paranoid. I wish you people would learn the distinction.

GATELY. He thinks you're holding out on him.

NATWICK. Can I help it if I've read books? Seen plays? Gone to the opera?

GATELY. You've been to operas?

NATWICK. Yes.

GATELY. I wouldn't let on if I were you.

NATWICK. What should I do?

GATELY. Why don't you make friends with Silvio?

NATWICK. How disgusting. (*Pause.*) What do I have to do?

GATELY. First of all, loosen up. You make people nervous.

NATWICK. Why.

GATELY. You're uptight.

NATWICK. I am not uptight.

GATELY. You stand like you got a rod up your ass.

NATWICK. I'm from Great Neck.

GATELY. Hey, come to our planet sometime. Look. Snap your fingers. Act like you're cool. (*Natwick does so. Mechani-*

cally.) You look like someone put a quarter in you. Say, "Hey man, what's happening."

NATWICK. Hey man, what's happening? Ad lib.

GATELY. (*Pause.*) OK. We'll come back to that. (*Pause.*) I know, walk backwards while you're going forwards. (*Gately demonstrates.*)

NATWICK. What?

GATELY. Walk backwards while you're going forwards. All America's doing it.

NATWICK. Gately, I refuse to walk backwards while I'm going forwards. If you do that you stay in one place.

GATELY. All America's doing it. I know you've got to take an interest in Silvio's hobbies.

NATWICK. Like what? Child molesting?

GATELY. No. Mainly flashing nurses, kilts, men's underwear.

NATWICK. Men's underwear?

GATELY. Yes, that and — oh, here he comes.

NATWICK. I think I'm going to be sick. (*Silvio enters in a hurry.*)

GATELY. Hey Silvio, what's happenin', man?

SILVIO. Gately . . .

NATWICK. Hey Silvio, what's happenin', man?

SILVIO. Gately, I gotta talk to you.

GATELY. Sure, Silvio, but Natwick just said hello to you.

NATWICK. Hey Silvio, what's happenin', man?

SILVIO. (*Pause.*) Gately, it's Nurse O'Brian. She's been transferred. All week I been planning on flashing her. I got her on the list for Tuesday.

GATELY. So?

SILVIO. Today is Tuesday.

NATWICK. Oh man, what a bummer.

SILVIO. What's the matter with him?

NATWICK. Hey, Silvio: "What it is baby?"

SILVIO. Why's he talking like a spade?

NATWICK. I mean what is this jive about O'Brian leaving?

SILVIO. Jesus. What is your problem, Natwick?

NATWICK. No problem, baby.

SILVIO. Don't call me baby.

37

NATWICK. I think it's great the way you flash nurses. You got it down to an art form.

SILVIO. Exposing yourself is not an art form. It's disgusting. You ever flashed anyone, Natwick?

NATWICK. No.

SILVIO. So what do you know about it?

NATWICK. Nothing.

SILVIO. That's right. Gately . . .

NATWICK. Hey Silvio, you wanna know what kind of underwear I'm wearing?

SILVIO. Do I what?

NATWICK. Very tight jockey shorts.

SILVIO. (*Backing off.*) Hey, has he gone queer or somethin'? Jesus. First O'Brian gets transferred, now Natwick goes queer. Jesus.

NATWICK. Silvio —

SILVIO. Keep your hands to yourself, Natwick.

NATWICK. I just want to be your friend.

SILVIO. You remember the cup? I'll glue you, Natwick. I swear to God I'll glue you.

NATWICK. (*Terrified.*) Don't glue me! Don't glue me! Don't glue me!

SILVIO. Hey. It's just a little glue. (*Exits.*)

GATELY. Well. You blew it.

BLACKOUT

JOHNNY CARSON

The three men sitting staring out blankly, stultifyingly bored. Lights unnaturally bright.

GATELY. You wanna see my Duke Snider? (*Silvio accepts baseball cards.*) Silvio . . . If you could have one wish . . . what would it be? (*Long pause.*)

SILVIO. I'd be on Johnny Carson.

GATELY. . . . Why?

SILVIO. I might meet Charo. (*Pause.*)

NATWICK. Can I see the Duke Snider?
SILVIO. No. (*Long pause.*)

BLACKOUT

RADIO PARTS ARE DISAPPEARING

Gately fixing radio. Silvio with baseball glove.

SILVIO. Gately. How can you work for weeks on one radio?
GATELY. You've got to keep the incoming parts ahead of the outgoing parts.
SILVIO. Run that by me again.
GATELY. (*Looking around.*) Silvio. Radio parts are disappearing.
SILVIO. When?
GATELY. All the time.
SILVIO. You think someone's stealing them?
GATELY. Possibly.
SILVIO. You could be losing them.
GATELY. Possibly. Anyway I have to replace the missing parts.
SILVIO. Where do you get the missing parts?
GATELY. You can't just get parts. You have to steal — acquire — the entire radio.
SILVIO. From where?
GATELY. From Administration.
SILVIO. Have you done this?
GATELY. Yes.
SILVIO. How many radios have you acquired!?
GATELY. To date, 27.
SILVIO. I see. You're quite a little acquirer.
GATELY. I'm not discouraged. The main thing is to keep your incoming parts ahead of your outgoing parts. America was built on this theory. Silvio. The Free Enterprise system. And if one guy like me can make a radio work — then America works.

SILVIO. Interesting theory.

GATELY. It's simple really. It's just a question of incoming parts and outgoing parts.

SILVIO. Gately . . . I wish you luck.

GATELY. Silvio, thank you. (*They shake hands. Gately goes back to radio. Silvio steals a part.*)

BLACKOUT

TRANSITION

NATWICK LETTER

NATWICK. Dear Mother: Thank you for sending the guppies for my aquarium. However, please do not send anymore, because Silvio took them out last night and smashed all my guppies with a ballpeen hammer. Please send socks.

JACK PALANCE

Natwick alone. Silvio enters, unseen, comes up behind Natwick. Silvio is acting very strange. Silvio steals radio part from table.

SILVIO. Hello, Natwick.

NATWICK. (*Startled.*) I wish you wouldn't do that.

SILVIO. Where's Gately?

NATWICK. He's obviously not here.

SILVIO. Good. We can have a little chat.

NATWICK. (*Rising.*) I really don't —

SILVIO. Sit down.

NATWICK. Thank you. (*Pause.*)

SILVIO. Well it's been lovely getting to know you this Spring, Natwick.

NATWICK. Yes, I haven't known fun like this since the Tet offensive.

SILVIO. You weren't no grunt. You were a clerk.

NATWICK. Correct.

40

SILVIO. Hey, Natwick. What kind of name is Natwick?

NATWICK. It's my name.

SILVIO. No, it's not. I looked up your file. That's not your name.

NATWICK. . . . No. It's not my name.

SILVIO. Good. Now where did you get this name, Natwick, Natwick?

NATWICK. I used to . . . write poems under that name.

SILVIO. Natwick. Jeez. It's not a very poetic name. My point is, we all gotta know each other's names, know who we are or else we're fucked. We'll be like animals in the wild. We won't know what to call each other.

NATWICK. Silvio, are you stoned? Are you stoned? That's good 'cause when you're stoned you mellow out. Right? Mellow?

SILVIO. You know who people tell me I look like?

NATWICK. No.

SILVIO. Jack Palance.

NATWICK. There is a certain resemblance.

SILVIO. The thing is, I had this dream the other night about Jack Palance. I dreamed Jack Palance was the leader of a girl scout troop. And he was dressed like a girl scout. And you and me and Gately were members of this girl scout troop. And we knew Jack Palance was going to do something horrible to us . . . so we decided to sneak up on him. And it was dark, Natwick, very, very dark. And then we opened the door. And there in this room was Jack Palance in this huge green girl scout uniform. And all around were dead girl scouts. He had bitten off their heads and drained their blood. (*Pause.*) Well, what do you think of this dream?

NATWICK. Fascinating.

SILVIO. Yeah, I know. But I mean in the Freudian sense.

NATWICK. Oh. In the Freudian sense, I'd say it was very common.

SILVIO. Common.

NATWICK. Oh yes. I think everyone's had that dream. I know I have. (*Pause.*)

SILVIO. Man, you're a real day at the beach, y'know that? (*Pause.*) See dreams can be really . . . real. This confuses me. I get unconfused, I get out of here.

41

NATWICK. You can get outta here anytime you want.

SILVIO. I know that.

NATWICK. . . . Besides, I don't believe you ever had that dream. (*Pause.*)

SILVIO. You're from Long Island.

NATWICK. That's right.

SILVIO. Great Neck.

NATWICK. That's right.

SILVIO. Bet you had shirts with the little alligators on them.

NATWICK. Uh, huh.

SILVIO. Bet you had a summer home in the Hamptons.

NATWICK. Montauk, actually.

SILVIO. Montauk, actually. (*Pause.*) I picture your home overlooking the ocean. The water coming in and out. In and out. In and out.

NATWICK. That's the way it is when everything's working right.

SILVIO. You pussy.

NATWICK. What?

SILVIO. I'll bet your mother played mah jong by the sea.

NATWICK. What's my mother . . .

SILVIO. And you went to private schools where they all wore the alligator shirts.

NATWICK. Silvio. (*Silvio takes out a knife. Puts it under Natwick's neck, stands him up.*) Silvio. Don't. (*Silvio releases Natwick and walks off.*)

BLACKOUT

I CAN'T GO ON

Gately fixing radio. Silvio listening to radio.

GATELY. (*Rising.*) I can't go on! I'll never fix this fucking radio!

SILVIO. (*Going to him.*) What seems to be the trouble here, trooper?

GATELY. (*Near tears.*) I try and I try and nothing ever gets done!

42

SILVIO. Calm down. Take two deep breaths. (*Gately takes them.*) Now then, tell me what your problem is here.

GATELY. It's that damn radio. I'll never get it fixed. Parts keep disappearing! Silvio, there's something wrong with me. Here. In my head. I think I'm —

SILVIO. Hey, you're just having a bad day.

GATELY. I am?

SILVIO. Sure. Did I ever tell you the story of the first day when I realized there was something wrong with me? That I needed help?

GATELY. No.

SILVIO. Well, I woke up one morning in Cleveland. I was living with my sister at the time. It was a beautiful day. I looked out the window. And I remember thinking, Ohio is a party dip. Not long after I attacked my fellow workers with a tire tool.

GATELY. Did you do that?

SILVIO. Sure I did that.

GATELY. But you're psychotic.

SILVIO. Exactly my point. And see, I couldn't even repair a radio.

GATELY. Well, it's not easy.

SILVIO. Hell no, it's not.

GATELY. Radios are complicated things.

SILVIO. Of course, they are.

GATELY. They're a product of human evolution.

SILVIO. Gately. If there's one thing that's clear to us at this point in time, it is that man is making progress. Hell, a million years ago if a man wanted to hunt a dinosaur, he'd have had to use a stick. Today if man wants to hunt a dinosaur, he'd have a rocket propelled grenade. This is progress, Gately. This is the free enterprise system. Now are you going to let yourself be defeated by an inanimate object? You are not. You are going to go over there and fix that radio.

GATELY. Will you go with me?

SILVIO. Of course I will. (*They go to table. Gately sits.*) Are you ready to resume?

GATELY. I am.

SILVIO. As you do, remember: "The flesh of man can be torn, beaten and destroyed, but the human spirit abideth

43

forever and shall not perish."
GATELY. Who said that?
SILVIO. Casey Stengal. (*Gately works. Silvio steals another part. Silvio tosses stolen part in the air.*)

BLACKOUT

SILVIO PSYCHIATRIST #2

Lights up on Silvio in the psychiatrist's office

SILVIO. Doc, I am not afraid of women. Doc, Doc, you gotta trust me on this one. I am not afraid of women. You're talking theory here, I'm talking fact. You're talking books, I'm talking reality. I'm not afraid of women. (*Pause.*) Well. Yeah. Maybe I'm . . . nervous around women. You didn't say nervous.

BLACKOUT

TRANSITION

NATWICK. Hello there. This is your Entertainment Director . . . Tonight's movie is *Bigger than Life*, 1956, starring James Mason. The frightening story of a cortisone addict. It's very well acted. Barbara Rush is very good. (*Natwick gestures to roll the film.*)

LIBBY

Silvio and Gately. Sunset.

SILVIO. (*Thoughtfully.*) Women are more sensitive . . .

GATELY. . . . Than who?

SILVIO. Than men.

GATELY. Ah.

SILVIO. Like, they don't like it when you pee in your pants. (*Pause.*)

GATELY. Well, who does.

SILVIO. No. Look. When you spring a leak.

GATELY. Spring a leak?

SILVIO. It's an expression.

GATELY. You mean "take a leak."

SILVIO. That's what I said.

GATELY. You said, "spring a leak."

SILVIO. No one says "spring a leak."

GATELY. You just did.

SILVIO. I do not "spring leaks."

GATELY. Well, neither do I.

SILVIO. . . . Well, sometimes I do.

GATELY. (*Repulsed.*) You spring leaks? Where?

SILVIO. Well, you know, you take a leak, give her the 'ol flipperoni and you think you got it all. I mean, you know you got it all, you're positive. And then you get back to bed and y'know. You didn't get it all. Women hate that. Women. Boy. Sensitive. (*Pause.*) What kind do you want?

GATELY. What kinda what?

SILVIO. Woman. You want one that likes you or one that doesn't like you?

GATELY. (*Thinks.*) One that likes me.

SILVIO. Her high expectations will make you miserable.

GATELY. (*Thinks.*) One that doesn't like me, then.

SILVIO. Her low expectations will make you miserable.

GATELY. One without expectations, then.

SILVIO. They all have expectations. You have to get one with minimal expectations, but not so minimal that she hates your guts.

GATELY. How 'bout a nice girl?

SILVIO. Lots of expectations.

GATELY. How 'bout a blonde?

SILVIO. Millions of expectations.

GATELY. A Catholic girl.

SILVIO. An entire galaxy of expectations.

GATELY. This isn't easy.

SILVIO. Hell no, it's not easy. (*Pause.*)

GATELY. I had this girl.

SILVIO. When?

GATELY. Yesterday.

SILVIO. (*Shocked.*) What?

GATELY. I had a visitor.

SILVIO. (*Relieved.*) Oh, she was visiting. She was a visiting girl.

GATELY. Yeah.

SILVIO. Who was this girl?

GATELY. I was working on the radio when I heard someone say, "Hi Woody!" And I turned around and there she was. And I couldn't remember her name. So I offered her a chair. And we talked about the radio and all about this guy that sold used cars who wanted to marry her. And I asked her why she didn't. And she said she couldn't. And I asked, "why?" And she said, "you know why . . ." By that time I remembered her name was Libby. She said it had taken her four years to find me. And I told her how respected I was here, how everyone looked up to me here. Naturally, she didn't believe *that.* And, at the end, she wanted me to kiss her. And I couldn't remember how. So she kissed me.

SILVIO. *She* kissed *you?* What did you *tell* that girl?

GATELY. (*Firmly.*) I told her, "look, I'm not leaving here till I fix this radio and make America work."

SILVIO. Atta boy. What'd she say?

GATELY. Something real funny. She looked at me kind of sad and said, "come home." Isn't that funny? Isn't that funny? (*Hold.*)

BLACKOUT

KRULLICK

SILVIO. How are you this afternoon, Woodruff? My, what a lovely day. Breathe that air, trooper.

GATELY. You feeling all right, Silvio?

SILVIO. Of course, I'm all right.

46

GATELY. You've got that look on your face.

SILVIO. What look?

GATELY. The last time you had that look, you flushed the cherry bombs down the toilet.

SILVIO. Gately, I'm in love.

GATELY. I don't want to hear about your love life, Silvio.

SILVIO. Don't you want to know with who?

GATELY. No.

SILVIO. Nurse Krullick.

GATELY. Not Neanderthal Krullick. *(Silvio nods.)* She's the ugliest woman in the world.

SILVIO. Do you really think so?

GATELY. She's uglier than the guy in *Ben Hur* that got dragged behind the chariot.

SILVIO. You think so.

GATELY. Of course. At least the guy that had been drug around by the chariot had an excuse. But Krullick was born that way.

SILVIO. That's why she deserves my love more than the rest.

GATELY. What?

SILVIO. Ugly women appreciate love more. They want it more. Gately, there are thousands of women out there that are starved for love.

GATELY. Silvio, Silvio. You're so fickle.

SILVIO. Fickle? Me?

GATELY. Only last week you were depressed because time was running out for you to make it with Raquel Welch.

SILVIO. A mere infatuation. How can you compare Raquel Welch with Krullick?

GATELY. It's not easy. *(Natwick enters. Sits.)*

SILVIO. Good afternoon, Natwick.

NATWICK. Uh, good afternoon.

SILVIO. Is that a new robe?

NATWICK. No. It's the same one I've been wearing all spring.

SILVIO. Well, it looks very nice on you. *(Silvio walks away, looking off.)*

NATWICK. What's the matter with him?

GATELY. He's in love.

47

NATWICK. Who's the lucky girl?

GATELY. Nurse Krullick.

NATWICK. Not Neanderthal Krullick. She's the ugliest woman in the world.

GATELY. Do you think she's uglier than the guy in *Ben Hur* that got dragged behind the chariot?

NATWICK. Oh, of course.

SILVIO. Gately, this is it. Wish me luck.

GATELY. Good luck. What am I wishing you luck for?

SILVIO. I'm going to talk to Krullick.

GATELY. How? I don't think she speaks English.

SILVIO. The language of love is the same in any country. Besides, I've got to tell her exactly how I feel.

GATELY. That you love her?

SILVIO. Yes.

GATELY. Silvio, be careful. If Krullick thinks you're making fun of her she'll tear you limb from limb.

SILVIO. That's a chance I gotta take.

GATELY. Silvo . . . good luck. (*They shake hands solemnly.*)

NATWICK. Silvio—(*Natwick flashes Silvio the thumbs up sign. Silvio returns it. He exits.*)

GATELY. Did you hear the news about Silvio? Silvio's leaving soon.

NATWICK. What?

GATELY. He's going to live with his sister in Cleveland.

NATWICK. So . . . he's getting out?

GATELY. Yeah. Isn't it great?

NATWICK. Yes. Yes. That is great. How's the radio?

GATELY. Won't be long now. (*Natwick steals a radio part.*) Is it possible Silvio really loves Krullick?

NATWICK. It's possible.

GATELY. And that she loves him?

NATWICK. Well, it's really a question of being faithful.

GATELY. (*Thoughtfully.*) People can be faithful to one another. It's hard. But they can do it. (*Pause.*) The coyote does it . . .

NATWICK. What?

GATELY. The coyote mates for life. He's entirely faithful. He doesn't fool around. And he's got plenty of chances. I

48

mean—he's out there, under the stars, under the moon. And I'll bet he gets lonely. He howls.

NATWICK. Dolphins, too. They mate for life!

GATELY. Do they?

NATWICK. I think so. I think they do!

GATELY. Good for them.

NATWICK. It just goes to show you, Gately.

GATELY. What?

NATWICK. Love is a many splendored thing.

GATELY. Why . . . that's beautiful. Love is a many splendored thing. Did you make that up, Natwick?

NATWICK. Yes I did, Gately.

GATELY. I'm impressed. (*Silvio enters quickly.*)

SILVIO. I can't fuckin' believe it.

GATELY. What?

SILVIO. I can't fuckin' believe it. I was standing there waiting for Krullick over by the cafeteria.

GATELY. Yeah.

SILVIO. And I see her coming, and I was about to say something to her, when suddenly, out of nowhere, comes Gleason. And what do you think the son of a bitch has the nerve to do?

GATELY. What?

SILVIO. He flashes Krullick.

GATELY. Gleason flashes Krullick!

SILVIO. Can you believe that son of a bitch, right in front of my very eyes! He flashes Krullick!

GATELY. What? You give him a shot?

SILVIO. I was going to, but he turned around and hauled ass.

NATWICK. Gleason got away from you?

SILVIO. Gleason can move that wheelchair when he wants to.

NATWICK. Did you tell Krullick you loved her?

SILVIO. Natwick! Have a little sensitivity, would you? The woman had just been flashed by a horny paraplegic. Romance was the last thing on her mind. (*Pause.*)

NATWICK. I hear you're leaving soon.

SILVIO. Yeah. That's right . . . tomorrow.

GATELY. (*Shocked.*) Tomorrow?

SILVIO. I was gonna tell you. My schedule got pushed up.
NATWICK. Guess you'll be glad to get back?
SILVIO. Fuckin'a. Y'know, see the old neighborhood. Check it out.
GATELY. (*Trying to smile.*) Well, we'll give you a going away party.
SILVIO. Yeah. Sure. Look. I gotta go pack and everything. See you later. (*Gately and Natwick watch Silvio go out.*)
GATELY. (*Singing.*) "Mr. Bluebird on my shoulder." (*Natwick joins him. Both.*)
GATELY AND NATWICK. "Mr. Bluebird on my shoulder . . ." "Mr. Bluebird on my shoulder . . ." "Mr. Bluebird on my shoulder . . ."* (*Natwick exits.*)

BLACKOUT

MISFITS

NATWICK. Hello. This is your Entertainment Director, Pfc. Natwick. Tonight's film: *The Misfits* (1961) — "An unsatisfying but engrossing parable involving a disillusioned divorcee and her brooding cowboy friends. (*Boo.*) Starring Clark Gable. (*Boo.*) Monty Clift. (*Boo.*) And Marilyn Monroe. (*Cheers.*) Gee, they all died right after making this film. (*Silence.*) Just a little piece of trivia.

BLACKOUT

THE PARTY

> *Gately and Silvio are very drunk. A bottle of Canadian Club and two glasses are out on the table.*

SILVIO. I mean, am I right or am I right?
GATELY. You're right.

*See special note on copyright page.

SILVIO. You're damn right, I'm right. (*Pause.*) What're we talking about?

GATELY. Cleveland.

SILVIO. Yeah. I just don't want it to be like last time.

GATELY. Last time you attacked your fellow workers with a tire tool.

SILVIO. I know. (*Pause.*) Say, where's the asshole?

GATELY. Natwick's been in his room all day.

SILVIO. How come?

GATELY. (*Delicately.*) I think he's depressed 'cause you're leaving. (*Pause.*) You know Natwick.

SILVIO. Yeah.

GATELY. You worried about going to Cleveland tomorrow?

SILVIO. No . . . well . . . yeah . . . a little.

GATELY. What're you worried about?

SILVIO. I'm worried about that damned Protestant.

GATELY. What?

SILVIO. My sister married a Protestant. I mean, how do you talk to a Protestant.

GATELY. I'm a Protestant.

SILVIO. You're different. (*Natwick enters. He has been drinking heavily.*)

NATWICK. (*Despairing.*) A party. Of course. I might have known. No one invites me anywhere.

GATELY. Natwick, you know perfectly well I invited you.

NATWICK. I couldn't hear you. The door was locked.

SILVIO. What were you doing in there, Natwick? Holding your breath?

NATWICK. That's right! Insult me! I just came out here to give you this. (*Hands Silvio letter.*)

SILVIO. It's from my sister. (*He begins to open it.*) I'll read it later. (*Pause.*)

NATWICK. Well, don't anybody offer me a drink.

SILVIO. OK, we won't.

NATWICK. Who needs your party!

GATELY. C'mon, sit down here, Natwick. I've got a surprise for you guys.

NATWICK. I've got martinis in my room. I have many martinis in my room.

51

GATELY. Sit over here, Natwick.

SILVIO. I think he's drunk.

NATWICK. I am not drunk.

SILVIO. Tell the truth, Natwick. You drunk?

NATWICK. Go fuck yourself.

SILVIO. Natwick is *very* drunk.

NATWICK. I am not. Gimme a drink.

GATELY. OK. Wait. We don't have enough glasses.

NATWICK. That's all right. I brought my own. (*He lifts hand out of pocket. A cup is glued to it.*)

GATELY. (*Reprovingly.*) Silvio.

SILVIO. (*Good naturedly.*) Hey—a going away present. (*Silvio and Natwick are seated on opposite sides of the table.*)

GATELY. Now, put on your party hats!

SILVIO. Jesus Christ, do we have to?

GATELY. Yes.

NATWICK. (*Wrestling with his hat.*) Jesus Christ.

GATELY. Here. I'll give you a hand.

NATWICK. It's all his fault! Can't even put a party hat on.

GATELY. (*Adjusting hat.*) There. (*Becoming rather solemn.*) I suppose you're wondering why we're gathered here this evening?

SILVIO. To wear these little hats?

GATELY. We're gathered to say farewell and good fortune to our friend Silvio.

NATWICK. (*Giving a rasberry.*) FFFTTT.

GATELY. And to celebrate the completion of the radio.

SILVIO. (*Sober.*) What?

NATWICK. (*Sober.*) What?

SILVIO. Have you tried it?

GATELY. Not yet.

SILVIO. How do you know it's gonna work?

GATELY. I've decided it will.

SILVIO. Radios are very complicated things. Remember we talked about this.

GATELY. I know, but I've worked long enough on this. I can't work on this thing the rest of my life. So today I screwed up the back and said to hell with it, it's now or never.

SILVIO. It's never.

GATELY. What?

SILVIO. There's no way that radio can work.

GATELY. Why not?

SILVIO. Because I've been stealing radio parts.

GATELY. You? I knew it! I knew something was happening. Do you know how many radios I've had to steal to replace those parts?

NATWICK. I took some too.

GATELY. You what? Do you know what this means? Do you have any idea?

SILVIO. It means the radio won't work.

GATELY. It's true people are always stealing from me. It's horrible. I leave my room in the morning and when I return in the evening, it's been stripped bare. Last week someone stole my dirty clothes. Stole my dirty underwear. (*Pause.*) All my life people stole from me. Bicycles. Baseball cards. My shoes. Shit. (*Silence. Suddenly Gately gives a loud . . .*) I'M THROUGH BEING STOLE FROM! That's it. No more stealing from Old Gately! That's it. No more stealing. From now on . . . I'm giving it away. Take my shoes. (*Takes off slippers.*) Take my shirt! (*Takes off shirt.*) Take my pants! (*Takes off pants.*) Take it all! Damn vultures. (*Stands in rage and defiance in his socks and underwear.*)

NATWICK. Can we have your socks?

GATELY. Take the damn things. (*He takes off socks. Stares at the radio.*) And take the goddamn radio. (*He goes to the radio with savage intensity, grasps it, lifts it over his head. He is about to smash it into a million pieces when, miraculously, it comes on playing very loudly, "The National Emblem March." The scene turns from one of pain to one of dazzled awe. Softly, Gately places the radio on the table. Turns off radio.*)

SILVIO. Gately . . . you fixed the radio. You know what this means, don't you? (*Gately nods.*) So. When you thinking of getting out of here?

GATELY. (*Quietly.*) When they let me out.

SILVIO. You can get out anytime you want. You fixed the radio.

GATELY. I know.

SILVIO. A to B. (*Pause.*) Say, Gately, where you from?

GATELY. Georgia.

SILVIO. I know that, but where? What did you do there?

GATELY. Started out on a red dirt farm near Macon with my old man. He was a funny old guy. Big old hands. He couldn't seem to make nothing work. He fucked up everything he touched. He fucked up the farm, he fucked up runnin' a fruit stand. He fucked up workin' for the state. Finally, we moved to Birmingham. He said that's where people like him moved to when they'd fucked up everything. He went to work in textiles. One day I come home and there he was, in the middle of the afternoon, leaned up against the house. Them big old hands. That's when I joined the Army. I couldn't stand to see him fuck up no more.

SILVIO. Say, Gately, when you were a kid, you ever do the Tarzan yell?

GATELY. Sure. Everyone did the Tarzan yell.

NATWICK. I never did.

GATELY. Why?

NATWICK. I had asthma.

SILVIO. Stand up here, Gately. I'm gonna show you how to do the Tarzan yell.

GATELY. Hell. I bet I do it better than you.

SILVIO. Are you fuckin' kiddin' me?

GATELY. I ain't kiddin' you.

SILVIO. I used to win prizes doing the yell.

GATELY. Big deal.

SILVIO. I did the Tarzan yell at a Bar Mitzvah once.

NATWICK. Hm. Must have been reform.

GATELY. OK. Who goes first?

SILVIO. I go first. Give you something to shoot for. (*He does the yell.*)

GATELY. I'm not impressed. (*He does the yell. Unexpectedly, Natwick does the call.*)

SILVIO. (*Realization.*) Natwick.

NATWICK. (*Pause.*) I did the Tarzan yell, I did the Tarzan yell.

SILVIO. This calls for a drink. (*They pour drinks, solemnly.*) A toast . . . to Tarzan.

ALL. To Tarzan. (*They drink.*)

GATELY. To Cheetah.

ALL. To Cheetah. (*They drink and sit.*)

54

GATELY. Sometimes I wished I were in a jungle somewhere.

NATWICK. (*Nodding.*) You know all over Africa, apes and other wild things that climb are falling out of trees at an unprecedented rate.

SILVIO. Why?

NATWICK. Civilization. There's no place anymore for wild and wounded animals. There's just all sorts of ancient things that disappear. They get obsolete. Like the dodo bird. And elephants.

GATELY. And Indians.

NATWICK. And Indians.

GATELY. And salmon.

SILVIO. And grilse.

NATWICK. Did you know that the universe is collapsing? That's right. The universe is collapsing. The energy in stars eventually collapses in on themselves. Eventually the entire universe will collapse in on itself.

SILVIO. Where will it go?

NATWICK. Nowhere.

GATELY. What will be left?

NATWICK. Nothing.

SILVIO. There's gotta be something left.

NATWICK. Nope.

GATELY. A couple of little planets.

NATWICK. Not even a little card table and a little radio.

SILVIO. At least there'll be a lot of open space for development.

NATWICK. No. When stars collapse, they create a vacuum and suck space into it.

GATELY. There won't even be any space? (*Natwick shakes his head.*)

SILVIO. Jesus Christ, Natwick, no wonder you don't get invited to parties. You are the most depressive son of a bitch that ever lived.

GATELY. He's an asshole.

SILVIO. Gately! You've admitted it! You've finally admitted that Natwick is an asshole!

GATELY. Yes.

SILVIO. Now I can die happy.

NATWICK. Big deal. He admits I'm an asshole. I *am* an asshole. Even I'll admit that.

SILVIO. Natwick . . . even you will admit you're an asshole?

NATWICK. Of course.

SILVIO. That's wonderful! Let's all say it out loud. Natwick is an asshole.

ALL. Natwick is an asshole.

SILVIO. Louder.

ALL. Natwick is an asshole!

SILVIO. One more time!!

ALL. Natwick is an asshole! Gately is an asshole! Silvio . . . Silvio is an asshole.

NATWICK. (*Continues alone.*) Silvio is an Asshole! (*A contented silence.*)

SILVIO. Yeah, we said it. We said it. Natwick. How long is it gonna take for everything to start collapsing on itself?

NATWICK. Oh, trillions and trillions of years.

SILVIO. Natwick, then there's nothing to worry about.

NATWICK. There's not? OK. Goodnight.

SILVIO. I'm gonna be in Cleveland tomorrow. (*Reads letter.*) "My darling brother . . . "

GATELY. Look, Silvio, the sun's coming up.
By the shores of Gitchiegoomie
By the shining big sea waters.
At the doorway of his wigwam
In the pleasant summer morning
Hiawatha stood and waited.
All the air was full of freshness.
All the earth was bright and joyous.
Natwick, you awake?

NATWICK. Hm. Aarg.

GATELY. Look at the dawn, Natwick. When was the last time you were up this early?

NATWICK. Last week.

GATELY. Yeah?

NATWICK. I had diarrhea. (*Gately sees Silvio.*)

GATELY. Good morning, Silvio. See how the world looks

this early. All dewy. It's like Eden, Silvio. Listen. It's like Eden.

SILVIO. My sister don't want me. She's gonna have the Protestant's kid.

NATWICK. (*Pause.*) I'm sorry, Silvio.

SILVIO. (*Miserably.*) Yeah.

GATELY. Try not to be so miserable, Silvio.

SILVIO. Gately, I'm a fucking psychotic with his pecker blown off.

GATELY. Things could be worse.

SILVIO. How? How could things possibly be worse?

NATWICK. It could rain.

SILVIO. Lemme tell you guys somethin'. Big news flash. Whether it rains or not really doesn't make that much difference. It wouldn't change anything.

GATELY. It would ruin a perfectly nice day. Look at it, Silvio! This day is special. It's like no other day that's ever been. It's like no other day that will ever be. This day will never come again.

SILVIO. Promise?

BLACKOUT

THE END

PROPERTY PLOT

THE RADIO
Radio
Tools
Pocket notebook

I DON'T WANT TO TALK ABOUT IT
Newspaper

UNDERWEAR
Pair of underwear

FREE ENTERPRISE
Piece of wire
Screwdriver
Radio
Radio parts

SUPERIOR
Chess set

HUMANOIDS
Note cards

HEMINGWAY / PEACHES
Cigarettes
Lighter

DRESSING GATELY
Pile of Clothes
Shoes

NATWICK'S SUICIDE
Piece of paper
Bottle of pills
Bottle of liquor

THE CUP
Cup

JOHNNY CARSON
Baseball cards

RADIO PARTS ARE DISAPPEARING
    Radio
    Tools
    Baseball glove

JACK PALANCE
    Radio parts
    Knife

I CAN'T GO ON
    Radio parts

KRULLICK
    Radio parts

THE PARTY
    Bottle of Canadian club
    2 glasses
    Cup
    3 party hats
    Letter

NEW PLAYS

★ **MONTHS ON END by Craig Pospisil.** In comic scenes, one for each month of the year, we follow the intertwined worlds of a circle of friends and family whose lives are poised between happiness and heartbreak. "...a triumph...these twelve vignettes all form crucial pieces in the eternal puzzle known as human relationships, an area in which the playwright displays an assured knowledge that spans deep sorrow to unbounded happiness." –*Ann Arbor News.* "...rings with emotional truth, humor...[an] endearing contemplation on love...entertaining and satisfying." –*Oakland Press.* [5M, 5W] ISBN: 0-8222-1892-5

★ **GOOD THING by Jessica Goldberg.** Brings us into the households of John and Nancy Roy, forty-something high-school guidance counselors whose marriage has been increasingly on the rocks and Dean and Mary, recent graduates struggling to make their way in life. "...a blend of gritty social drama, poetic humor and unsubtle existential contemplation..." –*Variety.* [3M, 3W] ISBN: 0-8222-1869-0

★ **THE DEAD EYE BOY by Angus MacLachlan.** Having fallen in love at their Narcotics Anonymous meeting, Billy and Shirley-Diane are striving to overcome the past together. But their relationship is complicated by the presence of Sorin, Shirley-Diane's fourteen-year-old son, a damaged reminder of her dark past. "...a grim, insightful portrait of an unmoored family..." –*NY Times.* "MacLachlan's play isn't for the squeamish, but then, tragic stories delivered at such an unrelenting fever pitch rarely are." –*Variety.* [1M, 1W, 1 boy] ISBN: 0-8222-1844-5

★ **[SIC] by Melissa James Gibson.** In adjacent apartments three young, ambitious neighbors come together to discuss, flirt, argue, share their dreams and plan their futures with unequal degrees of deep hopefulness and abject despair. "A work...concerned with the sound and power of language..." –*NY Times.* "...a wonderfully original take on urban friendship and the comedy of manners—a *Design for Living* for our times..." –*NY Observer.* [3M, 2W] ISBN: 0-8222-1872-0

★ **LOOKING FOR NORMAL by Jane Anderson.** Roy and Irma's twenty-five-year marriage is thrown into turmoil when Roy confesses that he is actually a woman trapped in a man's body, forcing the couple to wrestle with the meaning of their marriage and the delicate dynamics of family. "Jane Anderson's bittersweet transgender domestic comedy-drama ...is thoughtful and touching and full of wit and wisdom. A real audience pleaser." –*Hollywood Reporter.* [5M, 4W] ISBN: 0-8222-1857-7

★ **ENDPAPERS by Thomas McCormack.** The regal Joshua Maynard, the old and ailing head of a mid-sized, family-owned book-publishing house in New York City, must name a successor. One faction in the house backs a smart, "pragmatic" manager, the other faction a smart, "sensitive" editor and both factions fear what the other's man could do to this house— and to them. "If Kaufman and Hart had undertaken a comedy about the publishing business, they might have written *Endpapers*...a breathlessly fast, funny, and thoughtful comedy ...keeps you amused, guessing, and often surprised...profound in its empathy for the paradoxes of human nature." –*NY Magazine.* [7M, 4W] ISBN: 0-8222-1908-5

★ **THE PAVILION by Craig Wright.** By turns poetic and comic, romantic and philosophical, this play asks old lovers to face the consequences of difficult choices made long ago. "The script's greatest strength lies in the genuineness of its feeling." –*Houston Chronicle.* "Wright's perceptive, gently witty writing makes this familiar situation fresh and thoroughly involving." –*Philadelphia Inquirer.* [2M, 1W (flexible casting)] ISBN: 0-8222-1898-4

DRAMATISTS PLAY SERVICE, INC.
440 Park Avenue South, New York, NY 10016 212-683-8960 Fax 212-213-1539
postmaster@dramatists.com www.dramatists.com

NEW PLAYS

★ **BE AGGRESSIVE by Annie Weisman.** Vista Del Sol is paradise, sandy beaches, avocado-lined streets. But for seventeen-year-old cheerleader Laura, everything changes when her mother is killed in a car crash, and she embarks on a journey to the Spirit Institute of the South where she can learn "cheer" with Bible belt intensity. "...filled with lingual gymnastics...stylized rapid-fire dialogue..." –*Variety*. "...a new, exciting, and unique voice in the American theatre..." –*BackStage West*. [1M, 4W, extras] ISBN: 0-8222-1894-1

★ **FOUR by Christopher Shinn.** Four people struggle desperately to connect in this quiet, sophisticated, moving drama. "...smart, broken-hearted...Mr. Shinn has a precocious and forgiving sense of how power shifts in the game of sexual pursuit...He promises to be a playwright to reckon with..." –*NY Times*. "A voice emerges from an American place. It's got humor, sadness and a fresh and touching rhythm that tell of the loneliness and secrets of life...[a] poetic, haunting play." –*NY Post*. [3M, 1W] ISBN: 0-8222-1850-X

★ **WONDER OF THE WORLD by David Lindsay-Abaire.** A madcap picaresque involving Niagara Falls, a lonely tour-boat captain, a pair of bickering private detectives and a husband's dirty little secret. "Exceedingly whimsical and playfully wicked. Winning and genial. A top-drawer production." –*NY Times*. "Full frontal lunacy is on display. A most assuredly fresh and hilarious tragicomedy of marital discord run amok...absolutely hysterical..." –*Variety*. [3M, 4W (doubling)] ISBN: 0-8222-1863-1

★ **QED by Peter Parnell.** Nobel Prize-winning physicist and all-around genius Richard Feynman holds forth with captivating wit and wisdom in this fascinating biographical play that originally starred Alan Alda. "QED is a seductive mix of science, human affections, moral courage, and comic eccentricity. It reflects on, among other things, death, the absence of God, travel to an unexplored country, the pleasures of drumming, and the need to know and understand." –*NY Magazine*. "Its rhythms correspond to the way that people—even geniuses—approach and avoid highly emotional issues, and it portrays Feynman with affection and awe." –*The New Yorker*. [1M, 1W] ISBN: 0-8222-1924-7

★ **UNWRAP YOUR CANDY by Doug Wright.** Alternately chilling and hilarious, this deliciously macabre collection of four bedtime tales for adults is guaranteed to keep you awake for nights on end. "Engaging and intellectually satisfying...a treat to watch." –*NY Times*. "Fiendishly clever. Mordantly funny and chilling. Doug Wright teases, freezes and zaps us." –*Village Voice*. "Four bite-size plays that bite back." –*Variety*. [flexible casting] ISBN: 0-8222-1871-2

★ **FURTHER THAN THE FURTHEST THING by Zinnie Harris.** On a remote island in the middle of the Atlantic secrets are buried. When the outside world comes calling, the islanders find their world blown apart from the inside as well as beyond. "Harris winningly produces an intimate and poetic, as well as political, family saga." –*Independent (London)*. "Harris' enthralling adventure of a play marks a departure from stale, well-furrowed theatrical terrain." –*Evening Standard (London)*. [3M, 2W] ISBN: 0-8222-1874-7

★ **THE DESIGNATED MOURNER by Wallace Shawn.** The story of three people living in a country where what sort of books people like to read and how they choose to amuse themselves becomes both firmly personal and unexpectedly entangled with questions of survival. "This is a playwright who does not just tell you what it is like to be arrested at night by goons or to fall morally apart and become an aimless yet weirdly contented ghost yourself. He has the originality to make you feel it." –*Times (London)*. "A fascinating play with beautiful passages of writing..." –*Variety*. [2M, 1W] ISBN: 0-8222-1848-8

DRAMATISTS PLAY SERVICE, INC.
440 Park Avenue South, New York, NY 10016 212-683-8960 Fax 212-213-1539
postmaster@dramatists.com www.dramatists.com

NEW PLAYS

★ SHEL'S SHORTS by Shel Silverstein. Lauded poet, songwriter and author of children's books, the incomparable Shel Silverstein's short plays are deeply infused with the same wicked sense of humor that made him famous. "...[a] childlike honesty and twisted sense of humor." —*Boston Herald.* "...terse dialogue and an absurdity laced with a tang of dread give [*Shel's Shorts*] more than a trace of Samuel Beckett's comic existentialism." —*Boston Phoenix.* [flexible casting] ISBN: 0-8222-1897-6

★ AN ADULT EVENING OF SHEL SILVERSTEIN by Shel Silverstein. Welcome to the darkly comic world of Shel Silverstein, a world where nothing is as it seems and where the most innocent conversation can turn menacing in an instant. These ten imaginative plays vary widely in content, but the style is unmistakable. "...[*An Adult Evening*] shows off Silverstein's virtuosic gift for wordplay...[and] sends the audience out...with a clear appreciation of human nature as perverse and laughable." —*NY Times.* [flexible casting] ISBN: 0-8222-1873-9

★ WHERE'S MY MONEY? by John Patrick Shanley. A caustic and sardonic vivisection of the institution of marriage, laced with the author's inimitable razor-sharp wit. "...Shanley's gift for acid-laced one-liners and emotionally tumescent exchanges is certainly potent..." —*Variety.* "...lively, smart, occasionally scary and rich in reverse wisdom." —*NY Times.* [3M, 3W] ISBN: 0-8222-1865-8

★ A FEW STOUT INDIVIDUALS by John Guare. A wonderfully screwy comedy-drama that figures Ulysses S. Grant in the throes of writing his memoirs, surrounded by a cast of fantastical characters, including the Emperor and Empress of Japan, the opera star Adelina Patti and Mark Twain. "Guare's smarts, passion and creativity skyrocket to awesome heights..." —*Star Ledger.* "...precisely the kind of good new play that you might call an everyday miracle...every minute of it is fresh and newly alive..." —*Village Voice.* [10M, 3W] ISBN: 0-8222-1907-7

★ BREATH, BOOM by Kia Corthron. A look at fourteen years in the life of Prix, a Bronx native, from her ruthless girl-gang leadership at sixteen through her coming to maturity at thirty. "...vivid world, believable and eye-opening, a place worthy of a dramatic visit, where no one would want to live but many have to." —*NY Times.* "...rich with humor, terse vernacular strength and gritty detail..." —*Variety.* [1M, 9W] ISBN: 0-8222-1849-6

★ THE LATE HENRY MOSS by Sam Shepard. Two antagonistic brothers, Ray and Earl, are brought together after their father, Henry Moss, is found dead in his seedy New Mexico home in this classic Shepard tale. "...His singular gift has been for building mysteries out of the ordinary ingredients of American family life..." —*NY Times.* "...rich moments ...Shepard finds gold." —*LA Times.* [7M, 1W] ISBN: 0-8222-1858-5

★ THE CARPETBAGGER'S CHILDREN by Horton Foote. One family's history spanning from the Civil War to WWII is recounted by three sisters in evocative, intertwining monologues. "...bittersweet music—[a] rhapsody of ambivalence...in its modest, garrulous way...theatrically daring." —*The New Yorker.* [3W] ISBN: 0-8222-1843-7

★ THE NINA VARIATIONS by Steven Dietz. In this funny, fierce and heartbreaking homage to *The Seagull,* Dietz puts Chekhov's star-crossed lovers in a room and doesn't let them out. "A perfect little jewel of a play..." —*Shepherdstown Chronicle.* "...a delightful revelation of a writer at play; and also an odd, haunting, moving theater piece of lingering beauty." —*Eastside Journal (Seattle).* [1M, 1W (flexible casting)] ISBN: 0-8222-1891-7

DRAMATISTS PLAY SERVICE, INC.
440 Park Avenue South, New York, NY 10016 212-683-8960 Fax 212-213-1539
postmaster@dramatists.com www.dramatists.com